Cat Quips

CONARI PRESS

This edition first published in 2006 by Conari Press,
an imprint of Red Wheel/Weiser, LLC
York Beach, ME
With offices at:
368 Congress Street
Boston, MA 02210
www.redwheelweiser.com

ISBN 1-57324-270-5

Printed in China by Leo Paper Products

13	12	11	10	09	08	07	06
8	7	6	5	4	3	2	1

"What is the use of a book…
without pictures or conversations?"

LEWIS CARROLL 1832 – 1898

The male body

"I love the male body,
it is better designed than the male mind."

ANDREA NEWMAN 1938 –

5

Laziness

" Laziness is nothing more than the habit of resting before you get tired. "

MORTIMER CAPLAN

Beauty

"I'm tired of all this nonsense about beauty being only skin-deep. That's deep enough. What do you want – an adorable pancreas?"

JEAN KERR 1923 – 2003

9

Shoes

*"I didn't have three thousand pairs of shoes,
I had one thousand and sixty."*

IMELDA MARCOS 1930 –

Cheap

" You have no idea how much it costs to look this cheap. "

DOLLY PARTON 1946 –

Lovely day

"It was such a lovely day I thought it was a pity to get up."

WILLIAM SOMERSET MAUGHAM 1874–1965

15

Overrated

" Success and failure are both greatly overrated but failure gives you a whole lot more to talk about. "

HILDEGARD KNEF 1925 – 2002

Resentment

"*Resentment isn't a magnetic personal style.*"

PEGGY NORMAN 1950 –

19

Keep your head

"If you can keep your head when all about you
are losing theirs it's just possible you
haven't grasped the situation."

JEAN KERR 1923 – 2003

21

Sit by me

"If you haven't got anything good to say about anyone come and sit by me."

ALICE ROOSEVELT LONGWORTH 1884 – 1980

25

Busy?

"Of course I don't look busy,
I did it right the first time."

SCOTT ADAMS 1957 –

keep the stork

"His mother should have thrown him away and kept the stork."

MAE WEST 1893 – 1980

29

Kittitudes

"I cannot abide the Mr & Mrs Noah attitude towards marriage; the animals went in two by two, forever stuck together with glue."

VITA SACKVILLE-WEST 1892 – 1962

Out o' town

"I couldn't help thinkin' that if she
was as far out o' town as she was out o' tune,
she wouldn't get back in a day."

SARAH ORNE JEWETT 1849 – 1909

31

Sparkling

> *"Her conversation was like a very light champagne, sparkling but not mounting to the brain."*
>
> GERTRUDE ATHERTON 1857 – 1948

33

Summer days

One of the fallacies of summer holidays is that you are going to get some serious reading done while you are lying on the beach.

NANCY STAHL 1937 –

ARROGANCE
AND HOW TO
ACQUIRE IT

Why bother?

"I've never had a humble opinion in my life.
If you are going to have one,
why bother to have it at all."

JOAN BAEZ 1941 –

39

Laugh

"Laugh and the world laughs with you; snore and you snore alone."

ANTHONY BURGESS 1917 – 1993

39

One more

"One more drink and I'd have been under the host."

DOROTHY PARKER 1893 – 1967

Drinking

"Even though a number of people have tried, no-one has yet found a way to drink for a living."

JEAN KERR 1923 – 2003

43

Marriage

"I married beneath me, all women do."

NANCY ASTOR 1879 – 1964

45

Evil options

"When choosing between two evils,
I always try to pick the one I have never tried before."

MAE WEST 1893 – 1980

A pretty face

"It has been said that a pretty face is a passport.
But it is not, it's a visa and it runs out fast."

JULIE BURCHILL 1960 –

49

Mother knows best

"My mother said it was simple to keep a man,

you must be a maid in the living room,

a cook in the kitchen and a whore in the bedroom.

I said I'd hire the other two and take care of the bedroom bit."

JERRY HALL 1956 –

Purity

"I'm as pure as the driven slush."

TALLULAH BANKHEAD 1902 – 1968

55

Frighten the horses

" *It doesn't matter what you do in the bedroom*

as long as you don't do it in the street

and frighten the horses. **"**

MRS PATRICK CAMPBELL

My job

"I figure when my husband comes home from work,

if the children are still alive,

then I've done my job."

ROSEANNE BARR 1952 –

Temptation

" *The best way to get the better of*

temptation is just to yield to it. "

CLEMENTINA STIRLING

Be nice to people

"Be nice to people on your way up,
because you'll meet 'em on your way down."

WILSON MIZNER 1876 – 1933

61

High heels

"I did everything Fred Astaire did - except backwards and in high heels."

GINGER ROGERS